ON THE TRAIL OF THE VIKINGS IN BRITAIN

PETER CHRISP

FRANKLIN WATTS

LONDON • SYDNEY

© 1999 Franklin Watts
First published in Great Britain by
Franklin Watts
96 Leonard Street
London EC2A 4XD

Franklin Watts Australia
45-51 Huntley Street
Alexandria
NSW 2015
Australia

ISBN 07496 3228 3 HB
ISBN 07496 3591 6 PB

Dewey Decimal Classification 941.01
A CIP record for this book is available from the
British Library

Printed in Dubai, U.A.E.

Planning and production by Discovery Books Ltd
Editor: Helena Attlee
Design: Simon Borrough
Consultant: Tim Copeland
Artwork: Stuart Carter, Stefan Chabluk, Richard Sutton

Photographs: Ancient Art and Architecture: pages 21
(top), 28; C M Dixon: pages 11 (top), 16 (top), 20, 24
(left); Crown Copyright: reproduced by permission of
Historic Scotland: pages 10, 21 (bottom), 25 (top);
English Heritage Photographic Library: pages 4, 6, 7, 9
(bottom), Robert Harding Picture Library: pages 7 (top),
29 (top); Isle of Man Tourism: page 27; Lincoln
Archaeology: pages 12 (both), 13 (bottom); Alex Ramsay:
cover, pages 8 (left), 16 (bottom), 22; Shetland Museum:
pages 17, 26, 29 (bottom); Trustees of the National
Museums of Scotland: 18, 19; Charles Tait Photographic:
pages 18-19; York Archaeological Trust: 5 (both), 8 (right),
11 (bottom), 13 (top), 14 (both), 15, 19 (bottom), 23,
24-25 (bottom).

CONTENTS

WHO WERE THE VIKINGS?

The word 'Viking' meant 'sea robber'. It was the name given to people who sailed to Britain from Norway, Sweden and Denmark more than a thousand years ago.

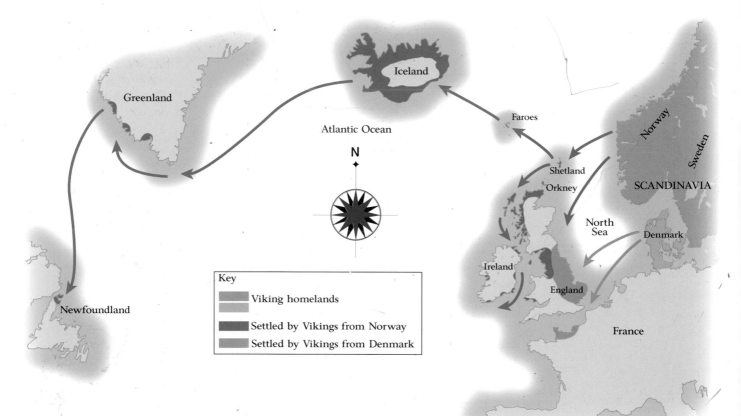

Greenland

Iceland

Atlantic Ocean

N

Faroes

Shetland

Orkney

Norway

Sweden

SCANDINAVIA

North Sea

Denmark

Newfoundland

Ireland

England

France

Key

Viking homelands

Settled by Vikings from Norway

Settled by Vikings from Denmark

◄ Some of the best Viking remains are stones carved with pictures and patterns.

▲ Britain was just one of the lands settled by the Vikings. This map shows the routes they took across the seas from their Scandinavian homelands.

The Vikings were great seafarers, building sturdy ships that they used for fishing and hunting seals and walrus. Gradually, the hunters made longer and longer voyages into the open sea. They raided new lands and brought treasure home with them.

Much of the soil in the Vikings' homeland was rocky and infertile. This made farming difficult. The Vikings began to search for better places to settle, where the weather was warmer and the soil richer. This was the beginning of the Viking Age.

The Vikings did not write books. In order to find out about them we have to look at the evidence that they left behind. By studying the remains of Viking houses, camps, ships, rubbish dumps and graves, archaeologists have been able to build up a picture of the Vikings and the lives they led.

At the Jorvik Viking Centre in York, a Viking street scene has been reconstructed, based on archaeological evidence.

▼ These delicately carved brooches were found in York.

VIKING CLOTHES
By looking at evidence such as scraps of cloth, brooches, shoes and caps, archaeologists have found out quite a lot about Viking clothes. The men wore tunics and trousers, and women had a long dress with a pinafore over it. Their clothes were fastened with belts or brooches. Spinning and weaving tools have also been found. This helps us to understand how the Vikings made their clothes from wool and linen.

THE EARLY RAIDS

The first Viking raids on Britain were aimed at the monasteries which were built on the coast.

The monasteries were places where Christian monks lived and worshipped God. The pagan Vikings saw them as a source of great riches. From about 790, they began to make frequent attacks from the sea.

The first Viking raid took place on 8 June 793. The monks on the island of Lindisfarne, in north-east England, noticed the square sails of strange ships on the horizon. The ships had sailed from Norway and they were packed with Viking warriors.

Key

✚ monasteries

➔ raids

795 date of raid

N

Shetland

Vikings from Norway

Orkneys

North Sea

Kingdom of the Picts

Dalriada

Iona ✚ 795

793 ✚ Lindisfarne

Strathclyde

✚ 794

Northumbria

795 ✚

✚ 795   ✚ 798
   832

Ireland

836 ✚

795 ✚

834

841

Vikings from Denmark

841

Mercia

East Anglia

835

✚ 823   ✚ 839   825

836

850

Wales

Wessex

789   840

838   850

The Vikings were armed with swords and battle-axes, like these raiders carved on a gravestone found at Lindisfarne.

6

VIKING LONGSHIPS

This is a reconstruction of a longship that was found in a massive royal grave in Norway. The Vikings who attacked Lindisfarne arrived in wooden ships like this one. They were strong enough to cross the stormy North Sea, but light and narrow enough to sail far inland up rivers, or to be pulled easily onto a beach.

The Gaia, a replica Viking ship, sailing along the coast of Greenland.

The raiders beached their ships and rushed towards the monastery. They killed some of the monks and captured others, keeping them for 'thralls', or slaves. They stripped the church of its gold and silver ornaments and then sailed away, back to Norway.

The raid had been very easy for the Vikings. The monastery was right next to the sea. It was full of treasure and yet the monks made no effort to defend it. They were holy men and they did not own weapons. It is hardly surprising that the Vikings returned again and again to raid monasteries on the British coastline.

The Vikings landed on this beach at Lindisfarne and attacked the monastery on the shore. The ruins in this picture are of a later monastery.

THE INVASION

In 865 a massive Viking army crossed the sea from Denmark and landed in eastern England. These Vikings planned to invade the land and stay for good.

For 14 years, the Great Army moved around England. The summers were spent fighting the English. Each winter, the army retired to a winter camp, like the one discovered at Repton in Derbyshire. We know from English writings that the Great Army passed the winter of 873-874 here.

This is Repton Church. It was built on the site of the Great Army's winter encampment.

WEAPONS

Viking warriors carried round, wooden shields. They were armed with spears, swords and battle-axes, weapons often found in Viking graves. A good sword was sometimes given its own name, such as 'leg-biter' or 'skull-crusher'.

These Viking weapons were found in York. You can see two swords, a spear-head and an axe-head.

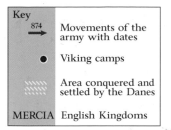

Key
874 → Movements of the army with dates
● Viking camps
≈≈≈ Area conquered and settled by the Danes
MERCIA English Kingdoms

N

NORTHUMBRIA
York
Repton
MERCIA
EAST ANGLIA
WESSEX

874
874
874
872
867
869
868
866
873
872
865
874
878
879
870
875
877
871
876

Archaeologists have found traces of a D-shaped ditch and earth bank near to the church on the site. One side of the camp would have been defended by a church, the ditch and the bank. The other was protected by the River Trent. This shows that the Vikings needed strong defences in order to survive in enemy territory.

To the west of the camp, archaeologists have found a grave holding the bones of 249 men, aged between 15 and 45. There was also a sword, an axe and coins dating from the early 870s - the time of the Great Army.

There were no signs of wounds on the bones, so the men cannot have been killed in battle. Perhaps they died of illness. Viking camps were such overcrowded, dirty places that diseases would have spread very quickly.

▲ This map shows the movement of the Great Army around Britain.

▶ These men are dressed up as Viking warriors. They are fighting a mock battle.

9

A FARMING SETTLEMENT

When the Vikings sailed west from Norway, the Shetland Islands were the first land that they sighted, after two days at sea.

There were already people living and farming on Shetland when the Vikings arrived. They were called Picts, and they had come from Scotland. Nobody knows exactly what happened to them, but in the 800s the Vikings took over their land.

Jarlshof, on the southern tip of Shetland, was lived in by Viking farmers for 400 years. You can still see the bases of the stone walls of the Viking houses. These remains show us that Viking houses had one long room where the whole family must have lived.

We know from other Viking sites that houses often had a bench around the walls which was probably used as a bed. A peat fire burned at the centre of the room. The Vikings lined the walls with earth to keep the draughts out.

The Vikings who lived in Shetland built long houses, as the remains of this house on Jarlshof show. Before the Vikings arrived, the only houses in Shetland were round.

The low, turf benches along the walls of this Viking house on the Isle of Man have survived.

The only thing that Shetland lacked was wood, which the Vikings needed to hold up their roofs. They probably used wood brought from Norway by traders. The roofs would have been thatched with straw or covered in turf.

Jarlshof was a very isolated place and the families who lived there had to make or grow everything they needed. The soil was good and they could have grown oats, rye and barley in the fields. Vegetables like cabbage and beans were grown near to the house. Bones found in the rubbish tip tell us that they also kept sheep, pigs, ponies and cattle on the fertile ground. Other bones show that they fished and hunted for seals.

At the Jorvik Centre in York you can see what the inside of a Viking house was like. Here, the family has gathered around the fire to keep warm and animals wander freely in and out of the house.

VIKING TOWNS

By the 880s, the Great Army had conquered much of the north and east of England. There were several important towns here, such as York, Lincoln, Leicester, Stamford and Derby.

Lincoln, which had been founded by the Romans 800 years earlier, was a perfect place for a Viking settlement. It was beside a river which meant that the Vikings could reach it by ship. It was also strongly defended by massive Roman walls.

▲ The Viking towns of the Danelaw, the name given to the area of England where the Danes from the Great Army settled.

▲This view shows archaeologists excavating the site of the Viking houses at Flaxengate in Lincoln in 1972.

During the 1970s, archaeologists dug at Flaxengate in Lincoln and found remains of houses where the first Viking settlers might have lived. They were wooden long-houses, each measuring around 16m by 5m. They had mostly rotted away in the dry earth, but a few black stumps of posts remained. Using this evidence archaeologists could work out what the houses had been like.

▲ An archaeologist's impression of what the Lincoln houses may have looked like.

Digging in York, archaeologists discovered the wooden walls and posts of Viking houses.

The Vikings had two ways of building in wood. They used either oak planks or wattle, which is springy twigs of hazel woven into a mat. Both types of house were found by archaeologists at Lincoln and at York. The Viking houses in York were much better preserved than those at Lincoln. The soil was very wet: wood lasts longer if it is waterlogged.

In Lincoln, many of the streets have names such as Danegate, Flaxengate and Micklegate. This is because the Danish word for street was '*gata*' or gate. Danegate means 'street of the Danes'.

Many everyday objects were found in Lincoln. These pottery weights were used by people spinning wool into thread.

VIKING CRAFTS

Viking towns were centres for trade and crafts. They were full of workshops, which were also the homes of the craftworkers.

The biggest Viking town in Britain was York, which the Vikings called Jorvik. Archaeologists digging here found all sorts of things that were left behind by craftworkers of the Viking Age. There were tools, materials and many of the things that craftworkers made. From this evidence we can tell that the Vikings were very skilled craftsmen.

Amber beads from a necklace found at Jorvik.

JEWELLERY
The York jewellers made rings, beads for necklaces and other ornaments. They used jet, a glossy black stone which came from Whitby, 70km away. Another material used was amber, which came all the way from Denmark.

Woodworkers in Jorvik carved bowls and cups. Leatherworkers made shoes, belts and sword sheaths from cowskin. Animal bones were carved to make pins, knife handles, whistles, ice skates and the counters used for playing games.

Some of the finds show that one workshop specialised in making combs from deer antlers. The antlers, dropped by red deer, would have been collected in the forests outside the town. The combs and comb cases were decorated with patterns made up of dots, circles and lines.

At York, archaeologists found this wonderfully well preserved Viking shoe. It is attached to an ice skate carved from bone.

IRON GOODS

Archaeologists have also found 200kg of slag in Jorvik. Slag is the waste left over when iron is heated. Iron was used to make weapons, tools and the nails needed for making Viking ships. It was a very valuable material. Old iron objects were heated and hammered to make new tools.

A collection of iron objects from York. Iron had dozens of different uses. Among these objects you can see belt buckles, tweezers and keys.

TRADE

The Vikings were great traders, sailing the seas and rivers of Europe in ships loaded with trade goods.

The Vikings sailed from their homelands with furs, soapstone and walrus ivory. They returned with slaves, wine and other goods.

Soapstone is a grey stone found only in Norway and Shetland. It is very soft which means that it could easily be carved. It is also fire-proof and hard wearing. The Vikings used it to make bowls, pots, oil lamps, ladles, weights for fishing lines, spoons and beads which they sold or exchanged for other goods.

WALRUS IVORY

We know about one Viking merchant called Ottar because he brought a cargo of walrus ivory to King Alfred of Wessex. The King asked Ottar to describe his homeland, and had his words written down. Ottar told King Alfred that he lived in the far north of Norway, where they hunted the walruses 'because they have fine bones in their teeth and their hides are very good for making ships' ropes'.

These chess pieces were made from walrus ivory. They were found on the Scottish island of Lewis.

Viking traders carrying soapstone from Shetland had to navigate the island's rough and rocky coastline.

Cunningsburgh in Shetland was an important soapstone quarry where there are still signs of Viking quarrying. You can see shapes carved on the rock face. These were left when people cut bowls from the quarry.

Although soapstone is not found anywhere in the British Isles except for Shetland, soapstone bowls have been found in York, Lincoln, and Dublin in Ireland. These bowls must have come from Shetland or Norway, which is good evidence of Viking trade.

Cunningsburgh is one of many important Viking soapstone quarries on Shetland.

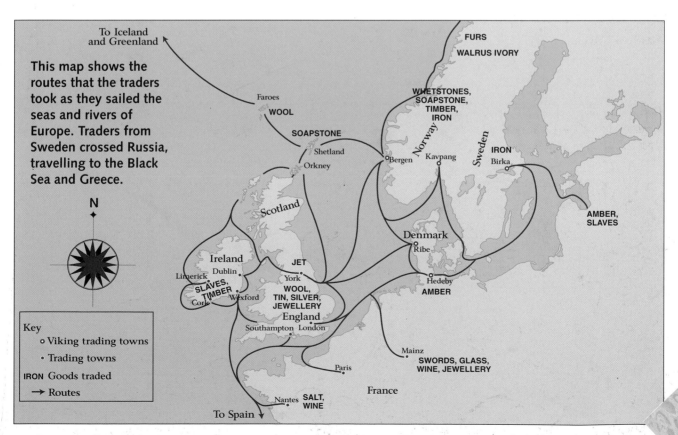

This map shows the routes that the traders took as they sailed the seas and rivers of Europe. Traders from Sweden crossed Russia, travelling to the Black Sea and Greece.

N

To Iceland and Greenland

FURS
WALRUS IVORY

Faroes
WOOL

SOAPSTONE

WHETSTONES, SOAPSTONE, TIMBER, IRON

Norway

Sweden

IRON
Birka

Shetland
Orkney

Bergen   Kavpang

AMBER, SLAVES

Scotland

Denmark
Ribe

Ireland
Limerick   Dublin
JET
SLAVES, TIMBER
Cork   Wexford
York
WOOL, TIN, SILVER, JEWELLERY
Hedeby
AMBER

England
Southampton   London

Mainz
SWORDS, GLASS, WINE, JEWELLERY

Paris

France

Key
○ Viking trading towns
· Trading towns
IRON Goods traded
→ Routes

Nantes   SALT, WINE

To Spain

17

SILVER HOARDS

There were no banks where money could be safely kept in Viking Britain. In troubled times, the safest way to look after money or treasure was to bury it.

Many Viking hoards, or treasure stores, have been found accidentally, often by farmers ploughing fields or workers digging the ground. In 1858, a boy was walking across the sand-dunes in the Bay of Skaill, Orkney, when he saw something glinting at the entrance to a rabbit burrow. He had discovered a Viking hoard. There was more than 7kg of silver, including Arabic and English coins as well as brooches and rings. The dates on the coins show that they were buried around AD 950.

Skaill Bay, Orkney, where the hoard was found. The ruins in the foreground are Neolithic. They were built before the Vikings came to Britain.

RING MONEY
In the hoard at the Bay of Skaill, there were 36 plain silver rings. These were known as 'ring-money'. They were worn on the arm by men and women – an easy way for Vikings to carry their wealth around with them and also show it off. When they needed money, they hacked pieces of silver off the rings. These pieces were weighed and used as money.

Brooches from the Skaill hoard.

Warfare was common in the Viking Age. There was fighting between the Vikings and the Scots, between the Vikings and the English, and between the different Viking groups. This fighting explains why people often buried hoards for safe keeping.

The mystery is why they were not dug up again by their owners. Perhaps the owners were killed in battle or forced to leave the area. Perhaps they simply forgot where they had buried their treasure.

Scales like this were used to weigh the silver used as money.

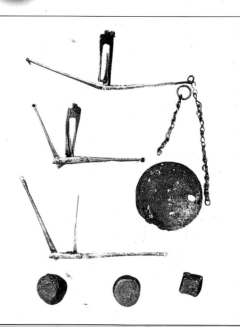

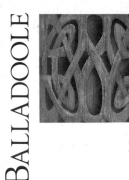

VIKING RELIGION

The Vikings believed in many different gods. Three of the most important were Frey, god of wealth and farming, his sister Freya, goddess of love and marriage, and Thor, god of thunder.

Odin was the most important god of all. He was the god of war, poetry and magic. He lived in a great hall called Valhalla, where he welcomed brave warriors who had died in battle.

This ship burial at Balladoole may once have had a mast, so that it could be seen from a distance.

The dead were often buried in ships or boats. Rich and powerful Vikings were buried in longships which were then covered with great earth mounds. Less important people were buried in small rowing boats.

At Balladoole on the Isle of Man you can see stones in the earth which make the outline of a boat. Archaeologists dug here and discovered that a real boat had been buried. Although the planks had rotted away, around 300 iron nails survived. The position of the nails showed that the boat was 11m long and 3m wide in the middle.

Although this is a Christian cross, found on the Isle of Man, it shows the Viking god Odin with his raven.

The bones of a man were found in the boat. He was buried with many belongings. There was a shield, an iron cooking pot, a knife and silver and bronze buckles. There were also burnt animal bones, including those from a horse, ox, pig, sheep or goat, dog and a cat.

Burials like this show that the Vikings believed in life after death. They must have thought that their new lives would be very similar to their old ones, as they would still need cooking pots and animals. Perhaps they were buried in boats because they saw death as a journey made by sea to this other world.

◀ This whalebone plaque was found in a woman's grave in Orkney. Similar plaques have been found in women's graves in Norway, but nobody knows what they were used for.

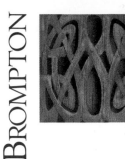

CHRISTIANITY

In Britain, Viking settlers learned about a new religion, Christianity. In time, many of them gave up worshipping Thor and Odin and started to worship Jesus Christ. They became Christians.

If you visit Brompton Church in Yorkshire, you will see some wonderful carvings left behind by Christian Vikings. They are called 'hogbacks' because they have arched backs, like pigs. Each is about 1.5m long, and is shaped like a Viking long house with roof tiles and rich decoration. At each end, great beasts are carved. There are bears, wolves and dogs wearing muzzles. Viking artists loved to carve animals and rich patterns.

Nobody knows for certain why these stones were carved. The fact that they are found in churches and churchyards suggests that they were Christian grave markers.

▼ It is thought that most Viking sculptures, such as these hogbacks from Brompton Church, were originally painted in bright colours.

The sites of hogback stones which have been found in many churches in Britain.

Key
• Single hogback stones
⦿ 5 or more hogback stones

When they became Christians, Vikings stopped burying their dead in ships and boats alongside their belongings. As Christians, they were taught that god would take care of all their needs after death. But perhaps the hogbacks show that they held on to some of their old ideas. They may have been seen as houses for dead people, with the beasts standing guard. The interlacing pattern may represent the interwoven, wattle walls of the Viking long house.

The Vikings may have got the idea for hogbacks from Christian shrines. A shrine was a container holding the bones of a saint. Shrines were shaped like houses or churches and they were covered in decorations.

A beautifully carved Viking cross in Middleton Church, Yorkshire.

WRITING AND LANGUAGE

The Vikings did not write books, but they loved stories, poetry and riddles. Viking kings and chieftains liked to have skalds, or poets, among their followers.

It was the skald's job to make up songs and poems to entertain people at feasts. We know the words of many Viking poems today because they were learned by heart and passed on until they were eventually written down.

The Vikings did have their own type of writing, called runes. There were sixteen letters in the runic alphabet, made of straight and mostly upright lines. Runic letters were used for carving short messages on stone, bone or wood.

The runes on this cross at Kirk Braddan on the Isle of Man read 'Odd raised this cross to the memory of Frakki his father.'

COINS

Viking rulers began to use the English alphabet when they minted coins. At first they copied English coins, which had Christian crosses and the names of saints on them. In the 930s, the kings of York began making coins with Viking pictures on them. These were signs linked with the gods: Odin's holy bird, the raven, and Thor's magic hammer.

Viking coins and the die used to make them, found in York.

These Viking runes were found at a Neolithic burial site at Maes Howe on Orkney. The Vikings had broken into the tomb and written their names, graffiti style, on the walls.

The biggest collection of runes in Britain is on the Isle of Man. In Braddan Church, you can see the remains of stone crosses carved with long curving dragons. These are typical Viking decorations. Along the edge of each cross, there is writing in runes.

In Orkney, there is a very ancient stone tomb called Maes Howe. Vikings broke into the tomb hoping to find treasure. They left graffiti - short messages scratched on the walls of the tomb in runes. Someone wrote 'Ingigerd is the loveliest of women' and 'The man who wrote these runes knows more about runes than anyone else west of the sea.'

The Vikings had all sorts of uses for runes. The owner of a sword might scratch his name on the blade. Carved on small strips of wood, runes were used to send short messages. Merchants used runes on wood to label the contents of sacks. Some Vikings used the letters for magic spells: a set of runes carved on a piece of animal bone was thought to have the power to heal the sick, or make someone fall in love with you.

VIKING LAW

At regular times, Vikings held big meetings in the open air to sort out arguments, punish criminals and talk over any important matters. The Viking name for a big meeting was a 'Thing'.

In Shetland, the meeting was held on a small island in Loch Tingwall, which means 'lake of the meeting place'. The island is still called Law Ting Holm - 'law meeting island'. It was joined to the shore by a stone walkway which can still be seen.

People came from all over Shetland to the meeting. It was held for a week in the summer, when the weather was fine and it was easy to travel. 'Things' were particularly important for the Shetlanders.

◄ Sites of Viking meetings or 'Things'.

▼ This aerial view of Law Ting Holm shows the stone causeway that links the island to the mainland.

TYNWALD PARLIAMENT
One of Britain's Viking 'Things' is still held each summer. This is the Tynwald, the Parliament of the Isle of Man. Every 5 July, the members gather on Tynwald Hill to give their agreement to laws passed in the previous year. The Tynwald has been meeting here for more than a thousand years.

The Tynwald still meets every year on Tynwald Hill on the Isle of Man.

There were no towns on the islands and everyone lived in farms that were scattered over a wide area. The 'Thing' gave the islanders a chance to see each other.

Only men could speak at the 'Thing', but they often brought their families with them. It was a big social event. People looked forward to seeing old friends again, and men and women went to find marriage partners. It was also a good place to do business, such as buying and selling land or slaves. The men might take this opportunity to organise a raiding or trading trip overseas.

THE END OF THE VIKING AGE

The year 1066 is often said to mark the end of the Viking Age. It was in that year that King Harald Hard Ruler of Norway tried to invade England. This was the last great Viking invasion.

This picture of the Normans who conquered England in 1066 is from the Bayeaux Tapestry. They crossed the sea in longships, like their Viking forefathers.

Harald failed and was killed in battle near York. Instead, England was conquered by the Normans, who were originally Vikings ('North men') who had settled in France.

Long after 1066, Viking languages were still being spoken in Britain. Over time, English speakers picked up hundreds of Viking words for everyday things. We still use these words, including law, husband, egg, take, happy, sky, ugly, knife, fellow, they, and window.

During the Up-Helly-Aa festival, the Shetlanders get ready to set their longship on fire.

We are still influenced by the Vikings who settled in Britain more than a thousand years ago. In some places, people remember their Viking past through festivals. The above picture shows 'Up-Helly-Aa', a fire festival which takes place on the last Tuesday in January in Shetland. Most of the islanders go to the capital, Lerwick, to join in the fun. Dressed as Vikings, they pull a specially built longship through the streets, finally setting it on fire.

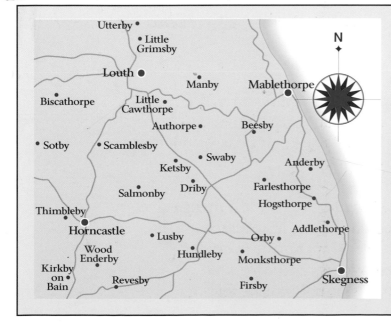

PLACE NAMES

Many of the places where Vikings settled still keep their Scandinavian names. These end in 'by' (farm), 'thorpe' (outlying farm), 'ness' (headland), 'holm' (island), 'beck' (stream), 'dale' (valley), 'wick' (harbour) and 'thwaite' (clearing). Look at all the Viking names on this map of Lincolnshire. The first part of each word often tells us the name of the farmer who lived there. Lusby, for example, means 'Lutr's farm'.

29

GLOSSARY

amber
a yellow stone formed by the hardened resin of ancient trees. It was used by Vikings to make jewellery

archaeologist
someone who digs up and studies ancient remains

craftworker
someone who uses their hands skilfully to make things

Danelaw
the area of England conquered and settled by Danish Vikings in the late 800s. It included several kingdoms, such as the Kingdom of York and the Kingdom of East Anglia

evidence
in archaeology, this would be physical remains that provide clues about the past

fjord
an inlet of the sea, with high cliffs on each sides, common in Norway and Sweden

longship
a long, slim Viking sailing ship, used for warfare

Neolithic
the New Stone Age

pagan
someone who is not a Christian or who does not believe in the generally accepted religion of the land

reconstruction
rebuilding

runes
Viking letters carved on wood, stone, bone or metal

soapstone
a soft stone found in Norway and Shetland, carved to make bowls and pots

Thing
a big open-air meeting of Viking free men, to sort out quarrels and discuss important business

thrall
a slave, someone who was owned by someone else

trade
the buying and selling or exchanging of goods

Vikings
sea raiders from Norway, Sweden and Denmark. The word is now used as a nickname for the peoples who came from these lands, in the years between AD 790 and 1066

warriors
fighting men

TIMELINE

AD 793   Viking raid on the island monastery of Lindisfarne

795   First raids on Scotland and Ireland

c. 800   Vikings settle on Shetland and Orkney

c. 840   Vikings found Dublin, in Ireland

860   Viking explorers reach Iceland, which they settle in 870s

865   Great Viking Army from Denmark invades England

867   Danes capture York

878   King Alfred of Wessex makes a treaty with the Vikings who settle in the area of England later called the Danelaw

c. 900   Vikings from Iceland sail to Greenland

901-937   English reconquer most of the Danelaw

911   Vikings found Normandy in northern France

980   New Viking raids on England

c. 1014   King Svein Fork Beard of Denmark conquers England but dies soon after

1016-1035   Svein's son Knut rules England

1066   King Harald Hard Ruler of Norway invades England but is killed in battle. Normans conquer England.

PLACES TO VISIT

The British Museum, Great Russell St London, WC1B 3DG: Viking finds from Britain and Scandinavia, including weapons and silver hoards.

Jorvik Viking Centre, Coppergate, York, YO1 1NT: A museum of Viking life in York, with a recreation of a bustling market, dark houses and a busy wharf, made more real with sounds and smells.

Manx Museum, Douglas, Isle of Man: Many finds from Viking graves on the island, and casts of Viking sculpture.

Jarlshof, Sumburgh, Shetland ZE2 9JN: Well-preserved Viking farming settlement.

Shetland Museum, Lower Hillhead, Lerwick, Shetland: Displays many of the finds from Jarlshof.

Vikingar! Visitor Attraction, Barfields, Greenock Rd, Largs, North Ayrshire, Scotland: A visitors' centre with displays on the Vikings in Scotland. Using computers, you can visit the battlefield at Largs and 'meet' the Viking god, Odin.

INDEX